NATIONAL GEOGRAPHIC

D0503573

More Places to Visit

Nick Bruce

There are many famous places to visit in the United States.

Have you been to the **STATUE OF LIBERTY**? It is in New York City.

The **Statue of Liberty** is one of the tallest statues ever built. It is a symbol of freedom. It is on Liberty Island in New York Harbor.

Have you been to the

WASHINGTON MONUMENT?

It is in Washington, D.C.

The WASHINGTON MONUMENT
is named after our first president,
George Washington.
It was built to help us remember him.

Have you been to the
GATEWAY ARCH?
It is in Saint Louis, Missouri.

The **GATEWAY ARCH** stands next to the Mississippi River. It's known as the gateway to the western half of the United States.

Have you been to the **GOLDEN GATE BRIDGE**? It is in San Francisco, California.

The **Golden Gate Bridge** is one of the largest suspension bridges in the world. The bridge hangs from cables suspended between two towers. The bridge connects San Francisco to northern California.

Have you been to
MOUNT RUSHMORE?
It is in South Dakota.

Mount Rushmore is a huge carving on a cliff. The faces of four presidents are carved into the cliff. They are George Washington, Thomas Jefferson, Theodore Roosevelt, and Abraham Lincoln.

Have you been to the **SPACE NEEDLE**? It is in Seattle, Washington.

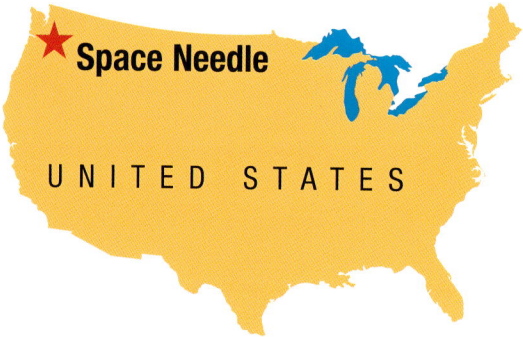

The SPACE NEEDLE is an observation tower. It was built for the 1962 World's Fair.

Have you been to these famous places?

Space Needle
Mount Rushmore
Statue of Liberty
Golden Gate Bridge
Washington Monument
Gateway Arch

INDEX

Gateway Arch	6–7, 15
Golden Gate Bridge	8–9, 15
Mount Rushmore	10–11, 15
New York City	2
Saint Louis, Missouri	6
San Francisco, California	8
Seattle, Washington	12
South Dakota	10
Space Needle	12–13, 15
Statue of Liberty	2–3, 15
Washington, D.C.	4
Washington Monument	4–5, 15